Number & Operations in Base Ten

Applying the Common Core Standards

Mathematics by Domain

4.NBT-1

4.NBT-5

4.NBT-2

4.NBT-6

4.NBT-3

4.NBT-4

We're all about student success!®

Developed by Robert T. Schwartz

ISBN 978-1-4204-7092-5
R 7092-5

RALLY! EDUCATION • 22 Railroad Avenue, Glen Head, NY 11545 • (888) 99-RALLY

Contents

Introduction 4
Reference Sheet 6

Vocabulary 8
These are the math symbols and vocabulary words for the domain **Number and Operations in Base Ten**.

Cluster: Generalize place value understanding for multi-digit whole numbers.

4.NBT-1 Modeled/Guided Instruction 10
Independent Practice. 12
Student Journal 16

4.NBT-2 Modeled/Guided Instruction 18
Independent Practice. 20
Student Journal 24

4.NBT-3 Modeled/Guided Instruction. 26
Independent Practice. 28
Student Journal 32

Cluster: Use place value understanding and properties of operations to perform multi-digit arithmetic.

4.NBT-4 Modeled/Guided Instruction. 34
Independent Practice. 36
Student Journal 40

4.NBT-5 Modeled/Guided Instruction. 42
Independent Practice 44
Student Journal 48

4.NBT-6 Modeled/Guided Instruction 50
Independent Practice 52
Student Journal 56

Introduction

Applying the Common Core Standards is a series of books that provides math instruction for the new Common Core Standards (CCS). Each book contains Modeled/Guided Instruction and Independent Practice problems for the Common Core Standards within a domain. The content within each domain is grouped by cluster. Each cluster contains one or more standards. The focus of this book is *Number and Operations in Base Ten*.

In addition to math problems, this book also contains journal pages for reflecting on your work and a list of vocabulary words. The list of vocabulary words are needed to better understand CCS math and will help you answer the types of questions found in this book. You should review the vocabulary words before answering any questions.

Using This Book

Each book in this series contains the following components:

Reference Sheet—To solve some math problems, you may need to use formulas or make measurement conversions. You may use the reference sheet to help you solve these problems. For some domains, you will not need to use the reference sheet.

Vocabulary—For each domain, there are some important words you need to know. You should review the list of vocabulary words in this book before you answer any questions. The vocabulary list for some domains may contain math symbols or units of measurement that are important to know.

Modeled/Guided Instruction—All of the problems in this book are grouped by Common Core Standards. Your teacher will show you how to solve two Modeled/Guided Instruction problems for each of the Common Core Standards, or your teacher will guide you as you solve these problems. Follow along as your teacher helps you solve each problem.

Independent Practice—There are four Independent Practice problems for each of the Common Core Standards. After your teacher has helped you solve the Modeled/Guided Instruction problems, you will solve the Independent Practice problems on your own.

Journal Pages—Following the Independent Practice problems for each standard are two journal pages. The journal pages are where you can write additional thoughts or questions you have about the problems you just solved. At the top of the journal pages are a series of questions. You should choose one of the questions to answer in the space provided.

Recording Your Answers

There are three different types of math problems that you will see throughout this series: multiple-choice, written-response, and gridded-response. However, only some domains contain gridded-response problems.

Multiple Choice—There will be four possible answers given. You must choose the best possible answer. Circle the letter next to the answer choice that you think is correct.

Written Response—If you are not given answer choices to choose from, you must write your answer. You may write in the book. Some written-response problems have more than one part. Make sure you answer each part and show all your work.

Gridded Response—Some of the domains contain gridded-response problems. When you solve a gridded-response problem, you must write the numbers for your answer in the boxes above the bubbles and darken the bubbles for each number in the columns below the boxes. If your answer is a decimal number, make sure the decimal is in the correct position.

EXAMPLE A:

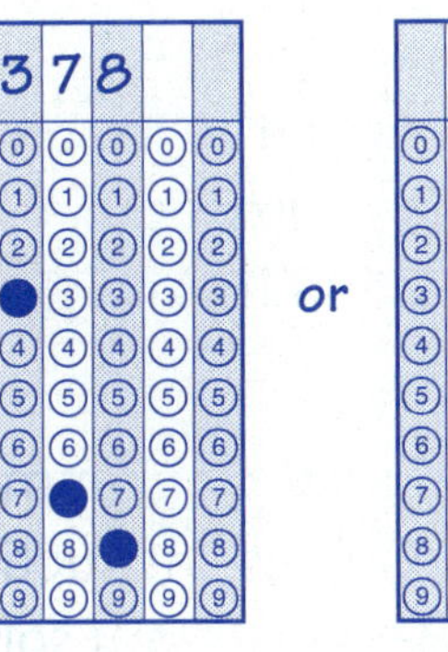

EXAMPLE B:

1 . 2 3

Reference Sheet

To solve some math problems you may need to use the formulas and measurement conversions on these two pages.

Formulas

Area

Rectangle: A = Length × Width

Square: A = Side × Side

Perimeter

Rectangle: P = (2 × Length) + (2 × Width)

Square: P = 4 × Side

Measurement Conversions

Length

Metric

1 kilometer = 1000 meters

1 meter = 100 centimeters

1 centimeter = 10 millimeters

Customary

1 mile = 1,760 yards

1 mile = 5,280 feet

1 yard = 3 feet

1 foot = 12 inches

Capacity and Volume

Metric

1 liter = 1000 milliliters

Customary

1 gallon = 4 quarts

1 gallon = 128 fluid ounces

1 quart = 2 pints

1 pint = 2 cups

1 cup = 8 fluid ounces

Mass and Weight

Metric

1 kilogram = 1000 grams

1 gram = 1000 milligrams

Customary

1 ton = 2,000 pounds

1 pound = 16 ounces

Time

1 year = 365 days

1 year = 12 months

1 year = 52 weeks

1 week = 7 days

1 day = 24 hours

1 hour = 60 minutes

1 minute = 60 seconds

*Note: Metric numbers with four digits are presented without a comma (e.g., 9960 kilometers). For metric numbers greater than four digits, a space is used instead of a comma (e.g., 12 500 liters).

Vocabulary

These are the math symbols and vocabulary words for the domain "Number and Operations in Base Ten." Review these symbols and words before you answer any questions.

Math Symbols

Symbol	What it means	For example....
>	is greater than	$16 + 19 > 34$
<	is less than	$12 \times 5 < 75$
=	is equal to	$21 - 7 = 14$
≠	is not equal to	$36 \div 13 \neq 4$

Vocabulary Words

place value

The value of a digit in a number based on its position. The value of each digit in a number can be shown using a place value chart. For example, in the number 752 the value of the 7 is 700 (7 × 100), the value of 5 is 50 (5 × 10), and the value of 2 is 2 (2 × 1).

thousands 1,000	hundreds 100	tens 10	ones 1
	7	5	2

rounding

A way to estimate or replace a number with another number that is easier to use. For example, you might round 99 to 100. When rounding to the nearest ten, look at the digit in the ones column. If it is 4 or below, the digit in the tens column remains the same. If the digit in the ones column is 5 or above, the digit in the tens column is increased by 1.

standard form

A number written as it is normally seen is said to be written in standard form. For example, two hundred thirty-four written in *standard form* would be 234.

expanded form

Expanded form means to express a number as the sum of the products of each digit and its place value. For example, $234 = (2 \times 100) + (3 \times 10) + (4 \times 1)$.

4.NBT-1

Cluster: Generalize place value understanding for multi-digit whole numbers.

1. Recognize that in a multi-digit whole number, a digit in one place represents ten times what it represents in the place to its right.

Modeled/Guided Instruction

Follow along as your teacher helps you solve problems 1 and 2.

1 In the number 6,666 how many times larger is the value of the 6 in the hundreds place than the 6 in the tens place?

A 6

B 10

C 60

D 100

2. Look at the following five numbers:

50,000 5,000 500 50 5

Write a number sentence that shows one of the five numbers is 100 times larger than one of the other numbers.

Independent Practice

Now solve problems 1–4 on your own.

1. In the number 143,695 the value of the numeral 4 is 40,000. If the numeral 4 was one place to the right, what would its value be?

   A 400,000

   B 30,000

   C 4,000

   D 1,000

2 Latoya saved 1,253 pennies to donate to an animal shelter. The value of the numeral 2 is 200. What would be the value of the numeral 2 if it changed places with the numeral 5?

3. In the number 67,754, what would be the result if the value of the numeral 7, in the thousands place, was divided by the value of the numeral 7 in the hundreds place?

4 Solve this problem by completing each of the following steps:

a) Write a number that has the same numeral, other than 0, in both the ten thousands place and the hundreds place.

b) In the number you wrote, what would be the result if the value of the numeral in the ten thousands place is divided by the value of the numeral in the hundreds place?

c) Will the answer for everyone in your class be the same even if everyone writes a different number? Explain your answer.

Your Math Journal

Choose One:

- Write directions for how to solve one of the practice problems.
- What questions would you like to ask your teacher to help you better understand the math you have just learned?
- Write two math problems that are similar to the ones you have just solved.
- What is something you would like to do or learn about in math class?

Cluster: Generalize place value understanding for multi-digit whole numbers.

2. Read and write multi-digit whole numbers using base-ten numerals, number names, and expanded form. Compare two multi-digit numbers based on meanings of the digits in each place, using >, =, and < symbols to record the results of comparisons.

Modeled/Guided Instruction

Follow along as your teacher helps you solve problems 1 and 2.

1 Which of the following is the correct way to use words to write 9,806?

A nine thousand eight hundred six

B nine thousand eight hundred sixty

C nine thousand eight hundred sixty-six

D ninety-eight thousand six

2. Write the number thirteen thousand eight hundred fifty-one in expanded form.

Independent Practice

Now solve problems 1–4 on your own.

1 The height of Kangto Mountain is twenty-three thousand two hundred sixty feet. What is the height of Kangto Mountain written in numerical form?

A 2,326 feet

B 2,360 feet

C 23,026 feet

D 23,260 feet

2 In the answer grid below, write the number that is the same as $3 \times 10{,}000 + 9 \times 1{,}000 + 7 \times 100 + 5 \times 1$.

0	0	0	0	0
1	1	1	1	1
2	2	2	2	2
3	3	3	3	3
4	4	4	4	4
5	5	5	5	5
6	6	6	6	6
7	7	7	7	7
8	8	8	8	8
9	9	9	9	9

3. Write a number sentence that compares the values of the following numbers:

4,568 4,685 4,658

Use the < and > symbols as needed in your number sentence.

4. During a two-week vacation at the beach, Alberto collected 1,299 shells, Kwami collected 1,929 shells, and Kisha collected 1,209 shells. Create a chart that shows the number of shells each person collected from least to greatest.

Your Math Journal

Choose One:

- Write directions for how to solve one of the practice problems.

- What questions would you like to ask your teacher to help you better understand the math you have just learned?

- Write two math problems that are similar to the ones you have just solved.

- What is something you would like to do or learn about in math class?

3. Use place value understanding to round multi-digit whole numbers to any place.

Modeled/Guided Instruction

Follow along as your teacher helps you solve problems 1 and 2.

1 Which of the following shows the number 32,865 rounded to the nearest hundred?

A 33,000

B 32,900

C 32,860

D 32,800

2 Beth wants to estimate the number of people at the skating rink to the nearest ten. There are 127 people at the rink. What should be her estimate?

Independent Practice

Now solve problems 1–4 on your own.

1. Ms. Kim asked Tyler to round a number to the nearest hundred. He correctly answered 31,200. Which number might have been the number Tyler was given to round?

   A 31,149

   B 31,165

   C 31,251

   D 32,201

2 Daria drove 448 miles to her ski house.

a) Rounded to the nearest hundred miles, how far did Daria travel?

b) How many more miles would she have to had driven for the distance to be rounded to the next 100 miles?

3 The chart below shows the result of the bake sale at Charlie's school.

Item	Number Sold
Muffins	136
Cookies	118
Brownies	129
Donuts	115
Cupcakes	131

If the number of each item sold is rounded to the nearest ten, name two items that would appear to have the same total sales.

4 During a 5-day period from Monday to Friday, Mr. Roberts put boxes of candy on sale in his store. Rounded to the nearest 10, he estimated that he sold 190 boxes of candy over the 5 days. Create a chart showing how many boxes he might have sold each day.

Your Math Journal

Choose One:

- Write directions for how to solve one of the practice problems.

- What questions would you like to ask your teacher to help you better understand the math you have just learned?

- Write two math problems that are similar to the ones you have just solved.

- What is something you would like to do or learn about in math class?

Cluster: Use place value understanding and properties of operations to perform multi-digit arithmetic.

4. Fluently add and subtract multi-digit whole numbers using the standard algorithm.

Modeled/Guided Instruction

Follow along as your teacher helps you solve problems 1 and 2.

1. Find the difference for the following math problem.

316 – 185 = ________

A 131

B 231

C 271

D 501

2 Samantha had $226 in her bank account. Daniel had $89 in his. How much more money does Samantha have in the bank than Daniel?

Independent Practice

Now solve problems 1–4 on your own.

1. What is the sum total for 28 + 146 + 97?

   A 261

   B 271

   C 623

   D 1,396

2 What number do you get as an answer when you subtract 128 from 396?

3. What is the sum total for 3,465 + 29 + 203?

0	0	0	0	0
1	1	1	1	1
2	2	2	2	2
3	3	3	3	3
4	4	4	4	4
5	5	5	5	5
6	6	6	6	6
7	7	7	7	7
8	8	8	8	8
9	9	9	9	9

4 On Monday, Philip had $302. On Tuesday, he spent $193 and received a gift of $29. How much money did he have at the end of the day on Tuesday? Explain how you got your answer.

Your Math Journal

Choose One:

- Write directions for how to solve one of the practice problems.
- What questions would you like to ask your teacher to help you better understand the math you have just learned?
- Write two math problems that are similar to the ones you have just solved.
- What is something you would like to do or learn about in math class?

Cluster: Use place value understanding and properties of operations to perform multi-digit arithmetic.

5. Multiply a whole number of up to four digits by a one-digit whole number, and multiply two two-digit numbers, using strategies based on place value and the properties of operations. Illustrate and explain the calculation by using equations, rectangular arrays, and/or area models.

Modeled/Guided Instruction

Follow along as your teacher helps you solve problems 1 and 2.

1 Find the product for the following:

$$36 \times 27 = \_\_\_\_\_\_\_\_$$

A 102

B 324

C 876

D 972

2 Below are two groups of columns and rows, called arrays. Array #1 has 56 smiley faces and array #2 has 20 smiley faces. Fill in the blanks below the arrays to write a true statement about the difference between the number of smiley faces shown in each array.

Array #1

☺ ☺ ☺ ☺ ☺ ☺ ☺
☺ ☺ ☺ ☺ ☺ ☺ ☺
☺ ☺ ☺ ☺ ☺ ☺ ☺
☺ ☺ ☺ ☺ ☺ ☺ ☺
☺ ☺ ☺ ☺ ☺ ☺ ☺
☺ ☺ ☺ ☺ ☺ ☺ ☺
☺ ☺ ☺ ☺ ☺ ☺ ☺
☺ ☺ ☺ ☺ ☺ ☺ ☺

Array #2

☺ ☺ ☺ ☺
☺ ☺ ☺ ☺
☺ ☺ ☺ ☺
☺ ☺ ☺ ☺
☺ ☺ ☺ ☺

_____ × _____ – _____ × _____ = 36

Independent Practice

Now solve problems 1–4 on your own.

1. Multiply the following numbers:

$$3{,}261 \times 6$$

What is their product?

A 15,976

B 18,226

C 18,566

D 19,566

2. Write down the steps to find the product of 47×39. Then, write your answer.

3 Find the area of the rectangular garden shown below.

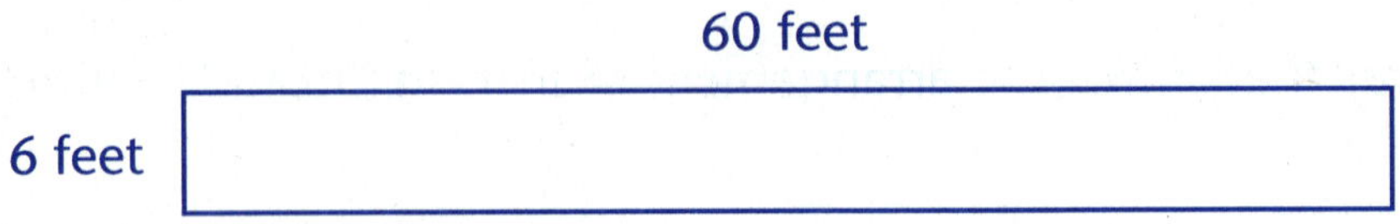

60 feet

6 feet

4 The auditorium at the Peach Street Elementary School has 16 rows of seats with 14 seats in each row.

a) Draw an array that shows the arrangement of seats in the auditorium.

b) Based on this seating arrangement, what is the greatest number of tickets that can be sold for the Spring Concert?

Your Math Journal

Choose One:

- Write directions for how to solve one of the practice problems.

- What questions would you like to ask your teacher to help you better understand the math you have just learned?

- Write two math problems that are similar to the ones you have just solved.

- What is something you would like to do or learn about in math class?

Cluster: Use place value understanding and properties of operations to perform multi-digit arithmetic.

6. Find whole-number quotients and remainders with up to four-digit dividends and one-digit divisors, using strategies based on place value, the properties of operations, and/or the relationship between multiplication and division. Illustrate and explain the calculation by using equations, rectangular arrays, and/or area models.

Modeled/Guided Instruction

Follow along as your teacher helps you solve problems 1 and 2.

1. A bin of oranges contains 464 oranges. The oranges from the bin will be packed into 8 crates. Each crate holds the same number of oranges. How many oranges will be packed into each crate?

   A 48

   B 58

   C 64

   D 72

2 Solve the division problem shown below. Then show how you can check your answer.

$$3{,}628 \div 9$$

Independent Practice

Now solve problems 1–4 on your own.

1. Find the quotient for the following math problem.

$$372 \div 6 = \_\_\_\_\_\_\_\_$$

A 56

B 62

C 72

D 76

2 Look at the math problem below.

$$5{,}819 \div 7 = \underline{\hspace{2cm}}$$

a) What is the quotient and remainder for this math problem?

b) Check your answer.

3 The area of Jason's living room is 171 square feet. As shown below, the width of the room is 9 feet.

What is the length of the living room?

4 Carl was asked to divide the array below by 3.

a) Show or explain what Carl must do. How can the array be divided into 3 equal parts?

b) How many small triangles would be in each part after the array is divided by 3?

Your Math Journal

Choose One:

- Write directions for how to solve one of the practice problems.
- What questions would you like to ask your teacher to help you better understand the math you have just learned?
- Write two math problems that are similar to the ones you have just solved.
- What is something you would like to do or learn about in math class?